ALSO BY FRANZ WRIGHT

Poetry

Earlier Poems (2007)

God's Silence (2006)

Walking to Martha's Vineyard (2003)

The Beforelife (2001)

Ill Lit (1998)

Rorschach Test (1995)

The Night World & the Word Night (1993)

Entry in an Unknown Hand (1989)

The One Whose Eyes Open When You Close Your Eyes (1982)

The Earth Without You (1980)

Translations

The Unknown Rilke: Expanded Edition (1991)

No Siege Is Absolute: Versions of René Char (1984)

The Unknown Rilke (1983)

The Life of Mary (poems by Rainer Maria Rilke) (1981)

Jarmila. Flies: 10 Prose Poems by Erica Pedretti (1976)

Wheeling Motel

Wheeling Motel

Poems

FRANZ WRIGHT

Alfred A. Knopf New York 2011

THIS IS A BORZOI BOOK
PUBLISHED BY ALFRED A. KNOPF

www.aaknopf.com

Knopf, Borzoi Books, and the colophon are registered trademarks of
Random House, Inc.

Library of Congress Cataloging-in-Publication Data
Wright, Franz, [date]
Wheeling motel : poems / by Franz Wright.—1st ed.
p. cm.
ISBN 978-0-375-71147-3
I. Title.
PS3573.R5327W54 2009
811'.54—dc22
2009015559

Published September 15, 2009
First Paperback Edition, August 16, 2011

For David Young

He had reached that moment in life, different for each one of us, when a man abandons himself to his demon or to his genius, following a mysterious law which bids him either to destroy or outdo himself.

—Marguerite Yourcenar

A man writes much better than he lives.

—Samuel Johnson

A traveler,
let that be my name.
The first winter rain.

—Bashō

CONTENTS

Wheeling Motel

Another Working Dawn

The dreamer was still soaring high above an endless city.

(The whole place could go in the time it takes a struck match to
        ignite.)

He found himself sad to say drowning in sight of land.

Was revealed to possess a mannequin-like pubic region, nothing
        there but blank hairless flesh hallelujah.

Was entering the precise number of times children's voices are
        heard in Rimbaud,

scribbling in the margins something about a rainy doorway and,
        How could I ever have been bored.

Music told me early I should be filled with joy.

The sound of someone crying woke him up and it was him—

the exceptional instrument who took very poor care of itself,

the leaf who thought it was a tree.

Lover of words, illumination's death-mask.

And let's get one thing straight, they were never *about*.

3

Those lines, say, on stars:

the hell with the stars.

They were about perception of the stars.

He turned the covers back like a page that weighed ten pounds.

Book in no known tongue, book that would not exist, truly,
      could he have foreseen the misery it would cause.

But I ask you voice that is nowhere and everywhere—

What did not in time become a source of suffering?

Baudelaire

"When I have inspired universal horror
I shall have conquered solitude,"
he wrote in his journal, in his rented misery.

Interesting strategy. The person who wrote
this was an ill and wrathful man. One
who constantly strove to do better, composer

of a couple sad dope-sickness remedies—
Icelandic moss?—and the firm resolution
to pray every morning to God, his mother

and Edgar Allan Poe. Who made,
the splendid mind, to self, this note:
"Whenever you receive a letter from a creditor

immediately write fifty lines
upon an otherworldly subject,
and you will be saved!" (If not from the stepfool.)

His throne a wheelchair in an empty park;
the satanic baby, *enfant du mal,* and Mom
the true power behind it right to the end.

Evil isn't hard to comprehend, it is nothing
but unhappiness
in its most successful disguise.

Evil is hated and feared at least.
It is possessed, unlike mere misery,
of a dark glamour nobody pities.

Kyrie

Around midnight he took the oxycodone
and listened to Arvo Pärt's "I Am the True Vine"

over and over, the snow falling harder now.
He switched off the light and sat without dread

of the coming hours, quietly singing along;
he smoked any number of cigarettes without thinking

once about the horrifying consequence;
he was legibly told what to say and he wrote

with mounting excitement and pleasure,
and sent friendly e-mails to everyone, *Lord*

I had such a good time and I don't regret anything—
What happened to the prayer that goes like that?

Day One

Good morning class. Today
we're going to be discussing
the deplorable adventures
of Franz Wright and his gory flute.
Just kidding. The topic this morning

is an unparaphrasable logic constructed
from parallelisms and images
and held together, on
occasion, by nothing
but the magical non sequitur—

but the hell with that.
We should really examine
your life, the one you bought,
and what happened when you got home
and attempted to assemble it:

that disfiguring explosion
no one witnessed, no one heard,
which you yourself cannot recall,
and by whose unimaginable light you seek
to write the name of beauty.

Will

I don't want to see a doctor
I want to kill a doctor.

And this is my alone
song, it isn't
long.

Everything is fine
everything is good
everything is happening
precisely as it should.

I've made all the money
it takes to be poor
here.

From always the gift of impermanence
so I would be ready,
accompanied

by a rage to prove them wrong,
prove they picked the wrong child to torment,

and that I too was worthy of love.

Agony of death, agony
of birth
unreal;

things
as they are, and
nirvana
unreal.
The disappearance
of me, and
then later
sentience in general
from this close to
nonexistent
mote
will have
upon the cosmos
needless to say
no discernible effect—

Desire
and the body
born of desire;
fame and shame
unreal.
But this: one
strange alone
heart's wish
to help all
hearts, this
was real.
This
was indestructible.

I'm going now to the mansion long prepared for me:
the eye socket of a shot crow,
the sapphire
wind on water,
halls of hawk-visited shadowy
pines like Chinese characters
in an ancient poem
not yet written,
and of childhood
the snows.

Intake Interview

What is today's date?

Who is the President?

How great a danger do you pose, on a scale of one to ten?

What does "people who live in glass houses" mean?

Every symphony is a suicide postponed, true or false?

Should each individual snowflake be held accountable for the
       avalanche?

Name five rivers.

What do you see yourself doing in ten minutes?

How about some lovely soft Thorazine music?

If you could have half an hour with your father, what would you
       say to him?

What should you do if I fall asleep?

Are you still following in his mastodon footsteps?

What is the moral of "Mary Had a Little Lamb"?

What about his Everest shadow?

Would you compare your education to a disease so rare no one
        else has ever had it, or the deliberate extermination
        of indigenous populations?

Which is more puzzling, the existence of suffering or its frequent
        absence?

Should an odd number be sacrificed to the gods of the sky, and an
        even to those of the underworld, or vice versa?

Would you visit a country where nobody talks?

What would you have done differently?

Why are you here?

Why Do You Ask

I breathed on the window and made my initial.

It's true, and then there was the dream
of being present
at my parents' wedding.

That's right: I breathed
on a little black fly-
husk there on the sill
and it came back to life,
why?

My body is lying in bed
all this time,
I know that.

I can see.

You say it's been there for a while?
You have no idea.

Sketch for a Novel

Chapter minus two hundred and fifty
in which the author pays (and pays for it,
as always), a visit to one of the lost: I

dropped by the dark house with no furniture,
knocked, and was introduced to her mother,
a woman much younger than she was

who for obscure reasons known only to
no one had kept her from childhood on
locked in the oven, &c. At this time

they were living together, or (hard to tell)
dying, possibly from a mystery
disease called being lied to by my friend

each time she breathed: this obsessively honed
and devotedly mutual hatred and hissing
contempt, I bought it—who knows? Classic case

of the wound lying down with the weapon?
Who cares? I did awhile, driven by picturing
(though I would have preferred to live

rained on, under a bridge) what would happen
if harm came to one of them, should
indeed anything this side of murder

slash suicide occur, although if they did
it was anyone's guess which event would
come first. In a flash you could see it:

all hostilities concluded, and their own
miniature World War III's aftermath
and the all-out final progressive and

uninterrupted commercial-free
stone-cold muttering psychosis awaiting
lone survivor of this conflict, the end.

After Absence

God's words translated into human words
are spoken and shine
on a few upturned faces.

There is nothing else like this.

I will tell you what no eye has seen
and teach you to see
what no ear has heard—

Father

and,
vine
of my blood.

Forgive me
the harm I have done

Those who have harmed me
forgive . . .

They say what we are going to be
will not become clear
until he appears

and when this happens
we will become like him
for we will see him as he is.

They say become passers-through.

God is love
they say,
in human words.

Association

Dawns when I can't sleep I walk,
in thought, all the way
around Walden.

My father loved Thoreau, I wish
he could have walked there
with me once,

my hungover Virgil. Lying in bed
with a big ax
lodged in my head, I still hear him

as if from the next room
bumping into things and cursing.
Give us this day, he mutters,

our daily stone. Nice.
Can't blame him, though. This morning
can't sleep for missing him.

The Our Father

I am holding cirrhosis
with one hand and AIDS
with the other, in a circle

to recite the august simple prayer
you briefly took on tortured
human form to teach

us, here, below—
Utterer of leaves, most mysterious
author of water and light;

taker and restorer of oblivion, what will it be?
What final catastrophe sent
to wean me from this world.

With a Child

Look at us. (Something does.) Smaller than life.
Much smaller. A sudden wind blows
through the new leaves and they are gone;
time blows through your hair,
the river of the dead

whose name's forgiveness, very
small, a blue vein
in your temple. And the words
for these things are so terribly small;
and the world of those words

only slightly less mortal
than this instant of taking your hand,
of taking care to look both ways,
not to squeeze too hard, or be too aware
that no such mercy will be proffered

by a world that has no need
of words, or us. And in the meantime
here I am still, silently asking
for—what? You guessed it. Words,
my God, not in Your tongue; the way

the mad mutter to keep themselves company,
to keep themselves from thinking. Words. Once
they did to the world what love does! Now,
to quiet and conceal my sorry terror,
they're going to have to do.

Pediatric Suicide

Being who you are is not a disorder.

Being unloved is not a psychiatric disorder.

I can't find being born in the diagnostic manual.

I can't find being born to a mother incapable of touching you.

I can't find being born on the shock treatment table.

Being offered affection unqualified safety and respect when
          and only when you score dope for your father is
          not a diagnosis.

Putting your head down and crying your way through elementary
          school is not a mental illness, on the contrary.

And seeing a psychiatrist for fifteen minutes per month

some subdoormat psychiatrist writing for just what you
          need lots more drugs

to pay his mortgage Lexus lease and child's future tuition
          while pondering which wine to have for
          dinner is not effective

treatment for friendless and permanent sadness.

Child your sick smile is the border of sleep.

Abandoned naked and thrown to the world is not a disease.

She was unhappy just as I was only not as lucky.

Triptych

I

I can remember forgetting so much . . .
　　　　　　—St. Augustine

In bed again composed
a line of verse then dreamed
I woke and wrote it down, thereby
neglecting to wake up and write
the thing down, therefore
waking in a desolation deeper
than the one in which I'd finally gone to sleep—
It was going to be great, it was something
about the word cloud ineluctably
billowing (brainlike, as
Denis J. says somewhere), sailing
without seeming to billow or move (if you stared
you could see it, but then you'd have suffered
reentry into time) across the sky;
it had to do with falling
into the *o*
of devour, the *i*
in flight,
something . . .

II

The Thinkers: A Scenario

On the verge of and I'm talking close
and concrete intellectual proximity
to grasping how everything works at its most vast
and incomprehensibly small, of
overcoming time itself
and visiting the cosmos, they
taught a gorilla to talk and
then exterminated themselves, fulfilling the prophecy
of the best that the species could manage,
one wheelchair-bound being all brain
cracking lame jokes with his machine while
collecting the royalties from his Einstein for dummies;
the last in a long line beginning
with some three-thousand-year-old Greeks
who for no better reason than that they could
invented our ceasing's
inevitability.
The same guy I am chilled to recall
I years ago found myself standing right next to
looking at one of van Gogh's more obscure
glories in Boston's Museum of Fine Arts;
same sainted and famously pitied Dr. Strangelove
black hole gifted smart boy I heard in an interview
once describe the name of Christ
in terms of bedtime stories for children afraid
of the dark (and now they have plenty), and

perhaps he himself now knows otherwise—
but to the green planet, that Eden
of sadness and our sentient home,
what difference does it make?

III

St. Paul's Greek Orthodox Church
Minneapolis, 1959

Don't look up, Christ's concave golden gaze
unbearable, wholly
beyond, beyond
holy: taste
the gold scent and kiss
the icon laid open, one wing of a book, with
its following eyes and
closed eyelid-like mouth's
superimposed prints
of lips (as one white rose is
manifested in others, too
infinitely petaled)—this mouth
hiving unnumbered
kisses
of the by now long long dead . . .
I've come back to the church
of my mother, of
my own deceased six-year-old
self and his father

as usual absent, and
I look straight ahead and slowly walk
into Mary's all enfolding
labyrinth-unraveled blue
and white child's-drawn-
stars-haloed
gaze
made of birds' sleep
and word-light
and find
without seeking, by
smell and touch only,
HER—
she is home, waiting,
visible,
here.

At 54

An instant of lucidity, an hour
outside of time,
a life—

I glance at the left hand
unclenched in the sunlight
shining on my desk

and think of my friend's
recent cremation—
that takes a while. And I can't wait

to return to this chair
in which I am sitting, this
world, the one where

each object stands
for nothing at all but
its own inexplicable existence.

Waltham Catholic Cemetery

JORDY POWERS: 1948–2007

On Calvary Street in October
we have not done nothing with our lives—
walking along still honing some words
to a bright and anonymous
saying.

Across the Marist sisters'
crowy hill, the source
of the perpetual
stillness
we alone hear.

Down Calvary Street, where
I know the hidden
footbridge
to
and over you;

Calvary Street
where we go to visit
our family the strangers,
and nobody asks us
what we do.

Professor Alone During Office Hours

River as verb, that's the assignment, until the next time I fail
        you.

And did you know the snail sometimes sleeps for a year?

And you will survive, that's an order.

I know it is hard to picture, but I myself was once twenty
                years old for an entire year.

I thought it would never end, afraid of the mailman, afraid
                to hear the telephone ring.

You're going to work eighteen hours at a stretch, and like it—
                that's what I said to the mirror.

Drinking cheap vodka and taking little white pills like a trans-
                Canada truck driver.

When I'm dying I feel so alive, those were the very words I heard.

Voice that speaks sometimes
to and through children
and the dying:
hear me—

Tell me
what I have.
I mean besides Honey's Dead
in 1990 Chelsea, Mass.
where the sunlight is

a small yellow icon of thorns.

How I envy the snail.

The Problem

Pretty soon you won't be doing that to get high.

You'll be doing it to get dressed.

Your time-travel seminar will be meeting in room 250
                Tuesday three years ago.

Eine Kleine Death Musik.

You're fired, actually.

You weren't born that way.

And it didn't happen overnight, no, you had to work hard all
                your life to achieve it;

a power over you steadily increasing in direct proportion to
                disbelief in it,

to the very evident fulfillment of your greatest fear:

you're going to live. When you wanted to quit

you could not, and when you could—

When you could you weren't about to.

Günter Eich Apocrypha

A pretty girl asks
for my autograph,
delighted! Except
it's her cigarette
she wants signed,
then lighted. Think of it.
Whenever I do
I am for a moment
the happiest man.
I have seen
my end
and it is someone else's
body, breath, strange
inspiration.

East Window: Little Compton

And the second hand slows,
and your pulse, and the avalanche

waits, every terrible thing in the past,
for the time being: the winter

sunlight meanwhile comes and goes
across the sea of beaten lead

one instant and the next
(Achillean) of beaten gold

and next a diamond vast abyss of light
until it is mere ocean once again—

nothing in itself was ever
good enough. Though soon

things as they are will become far
more memorable than you can endure.

The Balance

for Alison

Disturbs me, like Simone Weil's
grandiose wish
to be "a crippled no one,"

this longing in myself
for heaven
or another life.

A black hole emits a B flat
sixty octaves below
middle C.

Two galaxies collide—
I think I need an aspirin.
Since 1985

the number of people
with no one to talk to
has doubled,

and here
I thought that I
was all alone!

There are two worlds,
dream and death.
Have you noticed

we always remember the good things
about the most terrible times;
and they come back to us in spirit

or we return to them, it's hard to tell,
when things turn terrible again.
They are all we can carry

and all we're allowed.
Finally
they *are* the spirit:

they are that bright
soul without margins, the speaker
of the text

in which words and experience
are one.
The one

whose still voice kept us
company, always,
when everything else turned away.

Für Elizabeth

Say I was one naked blind man carrying
this infinite blue mountain on my back,
and all I might have done for love's sake,
and my best words, written in sleep and forgotten.
Now I have laid them down.

Out of Delusion

In blue branches the moon feigning
coma all morning, always
fading, and drifting away
A book one wrote decades ago now
seems stranger than somebody else's

Of the slumbering
hand,
this change
ineluctable, cloudlike

I speak in the mask of the first person

Not as myself, not in the glory
of action, of experience
when time and dying stop

but as anyone in the in-between hours
the hours alone, or traveling, or waking in a strange room
or the moment when friends all fall silent, and each
gazes into his own past and his own end
That is what I meant, the way things look then

Music, silence, the word

I'd emulate
these little
candles just lit

for the newly
dead, enter
the endless, the
original words
which shine
from behind
and through words

and be through with them
through with all
words

So desperately tired of the long, long flight from God

One hourglass of eventual
cremation dust, thinking
Get me out of here

Riding the subway I glimpse myself
in the seat next to mine
in the adjacent universe
one urinous drooling but otherwise fine human
hamster attempting and repeatedly failing
to pour cough syrup into a spoon

Thinking *the sky is a river of souls*
as everyone knows
darkness and blizzards
come from the future
and the road is long
as the memory of a child

Thinking *I*
could not bear to know what I do

No one knows no one like I do

Sparrow at the gates of heaven
or maggot at the gates of heaven
there I am
with all the others
from the twentieth century of horror

And that is a beginning.

No Answer No Why

Everyone Lord who wakes up insane

with window and mirror wintry portrait of nowhere.

Everyone Lord who wakes up in a cell.

Everyone Lord who wakes up in the cancer bed.

Everyone walking the streets with no home and intense frowning
        features of feigned occupation, feigned
        destination.

Everyone whose soliloquy more or less translates I'm fine, my
        life is good, and I need no one

when in Love's eyes he is nothing but naked, helpless, blind,
        starving and lost.

What are we Lord if not that small dog last night wandering
        obliviously into heavy traffic smiling and hopefully
        trying to find his way home.

Blinding light that's backed by an annihilating darkness rapidly
        approaching.

The last startled lurch to escape taking us under its wheels—

There is more, there's the fleeting, the overhead clouds' shadow
          racing the car through the radiant wheat plains of
          Kansas and passing me, twenty-four,

back into daylight, gold lightning falling

along all 360° of Nebraska horizon, no radio for some
          time;

or the drive through the Rockies afraid as alone in a room with
          my speechless mother—

that didn't last very long, but

was distinctly eternal, in its hour: let's not forget this, what the
          hell,

brighter gifts of our brief being

here, the black and not-hereness oblivion split, the flash.

Long ago I pledged allegiance to the chosen damned, and yet.

Unwriting

The universe is mostly made of thought,
a few weirdly simple equations
known and still unknown.

Sentient beings are numberless
and I promise to save them,
when you are old and I am a story.

It is all contained
in a few words
written and unwritten.

Winter, thank God. I will wander
from room to room, window to window,
a fictional person gazing at fictional skies.

The Question

My full name is spoken
        over the water,

the black lake's still cumulus surface:

it comes across the field and bends the wheat
        in this utterly calm

voice neither threatening nor intimate: more

like a question being posed.
        Just so.

And I stop in the road listening for a long instant

and recognize the simple and familiar
        two-word sentence, asking

once. It's only going to say it once,

apparently; for now

it is just wind.

Northern Ohio, summer 1975: LSD

44

Approaching New York City

Gray wastescape
by mid-day
glare, a sort of
empty refrigerator light
everywhere—

Approach to New York through the South Bronx, vast
hives of home to the world
of death and breath, just like anyplace else
but different: the White House of God, maybe; mother-
like mountains or statues . . .

On the night Greyhound:
once in loose-fitting hospital gown you approached
and pushing the IV-stand before you down the aisle
stopped at my seat without looking, startling me awake.
(And white roses rapidly spreading like cold flames, over your
          eyelids, the endlessly uttered white petals.)

Approaching New York City
signifies, primarily, approaching you—always
has, your face
like the sky it is everywhere, at every
turn, though you're a prisoner of Not today

and taken far from me.
But I am on my way,

one way or another I will
come knocking as so many times before,
I won't be long:
oh I will once again
belong, I know it.

Address

Remember us, you not

yet here. Of the sparrow-colored
fields

of mid-November, we the
perceivers, the
sayers
and rememberers—

call us
to mind, say the words
in our name:

they are our name, who breathed

here in these underground cloud-
darkened wind-uttered
fields, and spoke
like you

each object's word.

Hospitalization

City he's lived in, alien
city he has died in:
in the back of an ambulance

locked
and unloaded
at Admitting, the lightless

Belmont pines towering
and swaying on this campus
of profoundest expulsion and failure.

His unspoken prayer:
I want to be a priest,
though all sense of Your presence forsake me. And

shall the least saving meaning,
too, be denied
the insane in this life?

You ought to see this place. Each
and every one of them
unreachable;

unable and
impossible
to love— . . .

When the nurse went away
with her needle,
stood at the foot of the bed

a dark
Mary.
A voice

saying, How are you feeling.

He was so high he was dead.

I feel just like a window with light coming through it, he
       said.

1996

December: Revisiting My Old Isolation Room

Lit window—
I know you're still up
there
(in the past)
where I left you

Scrawny starlings building
out of nothing hopeless shelter
in the snowy corner of
that window gone abruptly dark

I freely stand here
watching
while you burn
unheard
among the screaming, the

zombies, the pacers, the shit-fingerpainters and furious
        nocturnal soliloquists

A bone-freezing wind blows. My mother
always left a shot of whiskey out
for Santa Claus, someone confides
quietly
close to my ear
twenty years ago

I think someone had lit a candle for me
I am sure of it
with so few plausible causes
to justify the current
and remarkably convincing
impression of one of the normal
with which I now (most days) present. But

the unvisited

in dark churches,
                            by their families now
unmentioned:

wind, cold wind, they blow the candles out and haunt Noël.

Happy Oblivion

It circles awhile, I suppose, until at last
having found nothing green
it returns.

The holy dove of tongues on fire released—

The birthday cake, the ruined and vacant
sheets, the pilot lost
in a vast dopamine cloud.

Closed eyes
and lips that open hovering
on the verge of speech, the final

breath, also known as the infinite
hours which preceded the first,
at last released.

Night Flight Turbulence

Some things need to be done
in the dark by yourself.
I'm not saying it's right.
In the greenly lit restroom
I looked pretty ill, like
a vampire locked in
a confessional;
the drug had no effect
whatsoever, maybe
slightly more arctic and fearful.
Angel of meetings
long despaired of, poor girl—
we could put something together
to eat, or
watch an old movie,
you and me
friendless
in this winter city
glimpsed for a minute as far off
lights passing under the wing, just
two more cripples Jesus
never got around to.
One theory says
we won't remember dying any more
than being born.
Where can you go at this hour,
stay with me.

To a Boston Poet

Personality changes: astonishing, even
voice timbre and handwriting

altered, the face too
to a degree

though perhaps I hallucinate
that (but

if so
then which I)

These are good words
They were here first

Crimson twilight crow
November mansion desert snow

Aldebaran
Now rose-gray winter Fens, the

room
overlooking the end, that

knee-high mound
of dentures—

Toward the conclusion the music speeds up, then
slows

into eternity
which

having arrived, the time being
(once again) now

about five in the morning
I changed

into my very worst clothes
and heading east set out on foot

At this point the narrator's
faced with a decision

Retain his super powers
or take the medication, or

if we are travelers
and clearly we are

all homeless travelers
to follow the poor

shade of John Wieners up Joy Street
and into the white morning air.

My Pew

I love this
window
way in the back
in early gentian morning
down which light's long
labyrinthine whispers
reach my ear, I
would like to describe it to someone,
to myself, my blind companion—
        Why did I turn to this
        forsakenness again?
Are You
just a word?

Are we beheld, or am I all alone? And

as that little girl on the psych ward
recently asked her father,
When I am very old

can I come back
home, and
will you be there?

The Call

The whole house in darkness
but for the single
lamp burning
throughout the
night haloing
me: no one
here except me
and the voice
which goes
on and
goes on (the
mere sound
of her voice
rendering me
unhappier and
less intelligent): nobody
home in the whole nighttime
world but an ear
and a voice,
only me and
my mother, the knife
giving the wound
some more free advice. And
what the fuck is that
supposed to mean?
I try to imagine
how my own child might
well have depicted

his strange bungling
parent. Because
witness the way
all I say until now
reveals my true
colors: about two
or three bright
shades of
chickenshit. Who,
I want to ask, is
this guy talking
anyway, this
speaker (as he
is referred to
in poetry
workshops); this
voice with its
transparent strategies
for coming across
as nobler and more
unjustly assailed,
blameless
and harmless
than I, trust me, am
or was, or
ever will be: his
majesty the aggrieved
with his well-rehearsed
silences; the one
who's done vastly
more harm in his life,
incalculably more than

that lonely old woman
he has never missed
an opportunity
to torture with a shrug
of clearly feigned
forgiveness, and all
the while her voice
continues
haltingly, shyly
attempting to speak
through the night
of concern for
me, and between
the lines, hopelessly
trying to convey
apology
and sorrow
and getting, for
her trouble,
still,
no answer.

The World of the Senses

What a day: I had some trouble
following the plotline; however,
the special effects were incredible.

Now this, the

dreaming breathing body
lying right beside
my own, just think—

at any given instant
it might undergo a change so
enormous that nothing is left of it

but mere object, a thing
to be taken from me, visited once
or twice, before it disappears.

Solution

What is the meaning of kindness?
Speak and listen to others, from now on,
as if they had recently died.
At the core the seen and unseen worlds are one.

Passing Scenes (While Reading Bashō)

I am traveling by train
to the city,
           I am traveling
in brilliant sleep
into the past.

Meanwhile composing
a letter
to my inner no one.

   There were hives at the
edge of a wood.

The mind shines
   in the
    window.

The most beautiful house I ever died in.

Everything's imaginary.

When I hear the dawn gulls cry,
even in New York,
I long for New York.

At the Desk

A forest of roses had grown up around him.
(Time flies when you're dead.)
A thin brook of blood threaded through,

and one bird sang.
(Took secret pill.)
He lay alone and listened to it for a couple years;

then he got up and added a comma.
He has been considering deleting it again,
but he cannot move my hand.

Thirteen Lines

Beware, beware
the booky wood;
beware abrupt attack
by large packs
of ravenous back-scratchers:
I don't even know what that means.
Moth light, north night;
March skies,
future goodbyes.
Fate and its opposite,
hope. Her
ruined bird's nest hair.
That's better.

Abuse: To My Brother

Just what the world needs, another world.

Just what the world needed, another
sad child—

another tortured mind.

(No one is born sad.)

There's a gladness in everything
when it's first breathing, a
bright naïveté
and a will to be well—
They'll kill it and then go have breakfast.
Why just the other day

I was five, abandoned
to my own devices
in Minneapolis, summer
storm approaching
darkening
everything—me
looming over
that infant bird fallen
from its nest overhead, mesmerized

by this power, unhindered
by parents or God, to continue
stuffing grass into its blindly gaping beak
until at last the eyes filmed over,
turned lightless, and it ceased to be alive.

Wheeling Motel

The vast waters flow past its backyard.
You can purchase a six-pack in bars!
Tammy Wynette's on the marquee

a block down. It's twenty-five years ago:
you went to death, I to life, and
which was luckier God only knows.

There's this line in an unpublished poem of yours.
The river is like that,
a blind familiar.

The wind will die down when I say so;
the leaden and lessening light on
the current.

Then the moon will rise
like the word reconciliation,
like Walt Whitman examining the tear on a dead face.

The Face

for Mary

I love those ruined
horror-corroded
faces that become, when
they smile, suddenly
childlike as I
tend to shy
from the other
fixedly childlike
appearances of those who
have merely grown old,
and that's *my* problem. But
it was in a moment
of gazing at one of
the former, a
stranger's, at dawn
on a Greyhound as we
approached Cleveland
first passing through
an absurdly satanic
zone of now close
to obsolete industry
where a few of
those faces, maybe,
still labor. And

it came to me
all at once, sat
down beside
me, this
final and long
longed-for job:
to be unhappy
without doing
evil. And
this conviction
of another, a constant
shining face beholding
the world in the night, even
toward dawn when
I wake up alone, very
ill, far from
home and all
sense of its
presence
deserts me
completely.

"My Peace I Leave"

The next life will be darker than this so
we must prepare
a light.

Help me change.
Here on my knees
in the hell of my
heart,
on its cold star,
apart.

Because if we say we are your followers
while in reality walking in darkness
we lie and do not live
according to the truth and so
I won't lie, and I will live
according to the truth, acknowledge
I mostly live cut off
and walk in darkness.

Help me,
   I still need to know

there is a place,
the temple still stands,
the unknowable
housed,

the infinite
somewhere.

Help me find
the horizontal
portal, the misplaced
sky-blue
book, which is

peace.

The world didn't give me this
word, but

the world cannot take it away—

The Catfish

Little cloud of inaudible gnats
in a shaft of morning sunlight,
in the silent sitar-shimmer
blowing through billions of leaves
and their shadows, the middle-aged catfish

in Walden's emerald
shallows, who says
I have done my best work
since I quit writing—
God, what is the meaning of

this minute,
tell me, I ask you.
I have already been here
forever, he replies,
and think I'm going to stay.

Reader

The solitary reader sits
surrounded by space
at the departure gate.

The world inside the book.
The world outside
the world.

Our faces,
so unlike
the ones that play them on TV,

will soon be flying
through the air, the
blue upper light.

Bumming a Cigarette

First one in a year. I walk the streets as ever,
though suddenly it's fall again, the same one, always.
A strange dog stops and stares quite specifically at me.
There's a message, but no means of transmitting it.
Sooner or later, I'm telling you, even the pity will cut you down.

And you can only armor yourself in death wish for so long, the
blows are not muffled, it will save you from nothing;
and the idiot drive to go on, and actually be glad to go on,
keeps breaking through ruining everything, even
this last chance for some sort of peace.

My homeless friend who never speaks nods back at me, it is
a lot like looking in the mirror of what I actually am, the
mirror of what I will be again, or some such metaphorical
      horseshit.
And I think of my brother, and the life he is living at this
      moment,
and everyone fucked from the minute he set foot in this world;

I think of my father, the arrow aimed thousands of years ago
striking, abruptly, from behind—
how he struggled to his feet and staggered on awhile,
unendurable pain lodged in his throat for six months,
one more time: of my father who died

a middle-aged man, and of my brother
a middle-aged man who died as a child
and last, myself, died Everett, Mass.
in nineteen ninety-seven
and resurrected by the force of love for this brief time.

The Student

I saw the student crying
on the steps to my Beacon
Street classroom that darkly
bright October day—
the next thing I knew
I was sitting beside her
and asking if she might like to
tell me about it.
"No,"
she replied. "Thanks."
This was said with great kindness and tact
as if in answer to a child
who'd offered her his sucker.
"Save your pity for yourself,"
wrote Heine in his obituary
on his friend Gérard de Nerval.
"Do you have the faintest clue
what may well one day happen to you?"

Text Recalled from the Fragments of Rilke

Traveling through the night
he bowed his head
and lived there for a while, some far off light

across the fields
while saying his goodbyes
forever, knowing you can never stay,

to translate from words that come back to me
suddenly, traveling through the night.
It comforts me as once the homeless boy.

The Soul Complains

I'm sorry to say the author was not very well today.
Sometimes I wish he would just get it over with.
He played the second movement of Bruckner's 7th Symphony
about fifty times, and he played it too loud
but fuck the neighbors—

a little intelligence sanity and beauty
won't kill them. Then he burned his manuscripts
in an infantile fury, and so forth. Which
struck me as excessive, but who am I to judge?
I was never even born and I will never die.

Though he does carry on: I mean he does it all
Sadday night and right into Stunday morning,
before passing out for twelve hours. Then he resumes
his normal personality of a turnip,
drinks a thimble of coffee,

and goes back to work, designing
a new bomb
that leaves everything just as it was;
the pallid translation of something done
in fire when he was young.

To a Young Poet

The sick wolf wandered off
grazing
in his wound's limping shadow,
sidereally alone and immune
to self-pity,
with no need
to describe how he felt
and no need of doctors to die.
Dear Fear,
Fuck off—
I can write to Valzhyna.
Dear Valzhyna,
I woke up this morning
groping around for a pen
to write these words down
on my hand;
I don't know what they mean.
It's just what we do.
The wolf woke with steel teeth
of the trap laid by men
clenched on his wrist
and did what was necessary
and wandered off.

Eucharist

Not alone, in unseen supervision I walk, between
time of ingestion and time of departure;
undisturbed, unafraid, as all things are passing—
the still unidentified bird spoke:
who will remember? And why
should I, aging
Telemachus,
care?
I had my time.
I got to be there.

Irises in Rain

What have I ever done but leave—
I only came to leave. Now
let your perfect silence heal over me.
And evening came, and the boat

was out on the water, and you were alone
on the land; and you saw
that your friends were progressing
painfully, as the wind was against them.

And about the fourth hour of the night
you came to them, walking on the sea.
So God will cross infinite space in a minute
and stand by the deathbed, and quiet me.

Anniversary

1. February 2, 2008: Learning the Rosary

Birth is the first affliction
but there is no birth.
Birth is the beginning of endless affliction
ending finally in dying
but there is no death. This
has never been explained
to me in words, but
mutilations. I watch you
watching something
from the window and smiling
in fear. (Will I somehow
still know you?) I see you
fifty years from now.
God is still naming the stars one
by one. And I see you alone
pushing your shopping cart;
the sun outside, much like today,
is shining, but all
that is illusion.
But if all is illusion
what to make of the heart
being torn from my chest
and force-fed me? Nothing,
nothing at all, I guess, not
in the world, not in this one
and only world

of time, where
I have a bad feeling
I won't in that other
be able to see,
ever, your face; and with that
I am having a serious problem,
and still can find no words
for it, the star being
hidden, the one
that might have led me
back to where words
are, still standing
for all of these things
that don't use them
and don't need this
broken mouth—

2. February 2, 1988: Park Drive, Boston

Aldebaran.
Gray winter park. The
room overlooking the end—

Hour
when the commonplace
objects around you, the weather
and the light peculiar
to the time of dusk begin
gradually to take on an unknown but
disquietingly personal significance

Don't look for happiness in the world

Don't look for it
anywhere else

Don't look for it—

It's everywhere

Because I couldn't feel it
didn't mean it
wasn't there

It was

once, up at four in the morning
in 1961
before you ever were
to read, to have two
whole hours of my own
from that strange grade school world,
and two worlds

All the way to the part
where Athena
yanks Achilles by the hair
snapping his head back
to gaze upside down
into her eyes, her
gray invisible
eyes in the air

It was there
once in a glance
of feigned indifference at my watch
trolling some Combat Zone slasher flick
there in straightfaced exaltation, that
suddenly remembering
in eighteen hours and thirteen minutes
I'm going to see your face

Aldebaran. Now
rose-gray winter
Fens. The
unfurnished
room overlooking the

rear of the MFA's long vast white windowless
tomb of the unknown

veiled

increasingly in horizontal blizzard, one
inch closer

Now

let go, forget
all that

put the pen down, this time
shut up
and wait

in the wordless

the patience; it
will flash

again

Await

the desire
the delight
the

energy clear understandable

spirit to set out once more, maybe
for the final time
like Bashō

to go
on foot
and die into the

beyond image allegory correspondence

3. February 2, 1998: Reunion

The best years came to me at the end, and
the best years came to me at the end
how many men can say?

And I'd like to keep it that way:
and every day I'll get myself a taste
of being gone, I don't care what I do.

And every day, every last day of my life
I have to sit down and write something,
oh I'll write weirdly well, with each word

mirroring her, the mysterious quiet-
spoken beauty, the brilliant, remarkably
non-Euclidean blonde called my wife. But

how little say I had in what I said:
the best years came to me at the end, and
love, the next best thing to being dead.

Music Heard in Illness

Everything changes but the avant-garde.
—Paul Valéry

A few words are left us from the beginning.
Thank you, God, for allowing me a little to think
        again this morning.

Touch my face, touch this scarred heart.
Here,

touch this upturned face as wind as light.

So they labored for three or four decades
to turn the perfectly harmless word quietude
into a pejorative sneer.

Call no man happy until he has passed,
beyond pain,
the boundary of this life.

We were standing alone at the window when it
started
to rain and Schumann quietly.

That imbecilic plastic hive of evil.

When it started to

night, and you
turned

and said,
although you were not there, Night.

What do we know but this world.

And although I could not speak, I answered.

ACKNOWLEDGMENTS

Grateful acknowledgment is made to the editors of the following journals in which many of these poems first appeared: *Harvard Divinity Bulletin, Alaska Review, Vallum, Ploughshares, Keane Review, Great River Review, New York Quarterly, RealPoetik, MiPoesis, Salmagundi, Redivider, Christianity & Literature.*

"Passing Scenes (While Reading Bashō)," "Out of Delusion," "Why Do You Ask," "Günter Eich Apocrypha," "The Problem," "Intake Interview," "Waltham Catholic Cemetery," "To a Boston Poet," and "Night Flight Turbulence" first appeared in *Field.*

"Address," "Approaching New York City," "December: Revisiting My Old Isolation Room," "Wheeling Motel," "The World of the Senses," and "Sketch for a Novel" first appeared in *The New Yorker.*

"Music Heard in Illness" appeared in *Best American Spiritual Writing 2007.* "Passing Scenes (While Reading Bashō)" appeared in *Best American Poetry 2008.*

A number of these poems (sometimes in earlier versions) appeared in the chapbooks *The Catfish* (Marick Press, Grosse Point Farms, Michigan) and *Address* (Vallum Editions, Montreal).

What is a book of poems if not a collection, or commemoration, of one person's best and happiest hours? That's how I feel about it, anyway.

But a book of poems is also, in my experience, a collaborative venture. So as always, I wish to thank Elizabeth Oehlkers Wright for her close readings and generosity toward my work. These poems have benefited greatly from her many inspired suggestions.

F.W.

—

A NOTE ABOUT THE AUTHOR

Franz Wright's most recent works include *Kindertotenwald,*
God's Silence, and *Walking to Martha's Vineyard* (which won
the Pulitzer Prize for poetry). He has been the recipient of
two National Endowment for the Arts grants, a Guggenheim
Fellowship, a Whiting Fellowship, and the PEN/Voelcker
Award for Poetry, among other honors. He currently lives in
Waltham, Massachusetts, with his wife, the translator and
writer Elizabeth Oehlkers Wright.

A NOTE ON THE TYPE

This book was set in Monotype Dante, a typeface designed by
Giovanni Mardersteig (1892–1977). Conceived as a private type
for the Officina Bodoni in Verona, Italy, Dante was originally
cut only for hand composition by Charles Malin, the famous
Parisian punch cutter, between 1946 and 1952. Its first use was in
an edition of Boccaccio's *Trattatello in laude di Dante* that
appeared in 1954. The Monotype Corporation's version of
Dante followed in 1957. Although modeled on the Aldine type
used for Pietro Cardinal Bembo's treatise *De Aetna* in 1495,
Dante is a thoroughly modern interpretation of the venerable
face.

Composed by North Market Street Graphics
Printed and bound by Thomson-Shore Dexter, Michigan
Designed by Virginia Tan

Printed in the United States
by Baker & Taylor Publisher Services